CE   RY

Fern Green

photography by Deirdre Rooney

61 RECIPES AND
12 DETOX PLANS

TEN SPEED PRESS
Berkeley

CONTENTS

INTRODUCTION

Today our bodies are exposed to toxins from when we get up in the morning to when we go to sleep at night. They come in the form of chemicals, pesticides, hormones, and other pollutants, and can be found in our immediate surroundings from paint, lotions, carpets, furniture, and even tap water. Although our bodies have a natural built-in detoxifier that helps expel these toxins, the increase in these substances, particularly in our foods, is putting a great burden on our health.

The buildup of toxins in our bodies can have lasting effects on our health, causing our immune systems to become weaker. Mineral deficiency makes the condition even worse; it can result in a variety of symptoms, including lack of energy, headaches, weight problems, allergies, mood swings, and insomnia. To detoxify efficiently, we need to give our bodies some assistance in eliminating these harmful substances. A detox plan can help with this.

What is a smoothie detox?

A smoothie detox can give the body the time it needs to flush out the backlog of toxins. During a short detox, the body is able to cleanse, purify, and rebuild itself. A longer detox (of more than a few days) can result in deep cleansing at the tissue level, where accumulated toxins and wastes have built up. Short fasts, like three days or five days, are a wonderful way to rid the body of toxins and boost the system. They stimulate the whole metabolic process: excess weight falls off, your skin becomes clearer, your hair shines, and your eyes brighten as your intestines are cleansed and your essential organs release stored-up waste.

Who can smoothie-detox?

Smoothie detoxing is, for the majority of us, completely harmless, and anyone who wants better health and more energy can give it a try. That said, those with chronic conditions such as diabetes, heart disease, liver disease, or cancer, as well as the elderly and pregnant women, should always consult their doctor first.

How often can we detox?

This depends on you, and on what other commitments you have in your life. The frequency and duration of smoothie detox can vary, but one day a week is a good starting point.

What to drink during a detox?

The most powerful detox smoothies are fruit based and contain citrus. These are believed to be stronger intestinal cleansers than vegetable smoothies. However, a pure fruit detox may leave you feeling a bit off. This book has a mix of fruit and vegetable smoothies. Drink plenty of filtered or bottled water and herbal teas throughout your detox day.

WHAT EQUIPMENT DO YOU NEED?

Whether you are new to juicing or you are a regular smoothie maker, it's vital that you have the right equipment. Juicers are great for juices—they can create juice from all fruit and most vegetables—but to make smoothies and nut milks, you need a good blender.

Your blender

With so many models on the market, you can shop around to find one that suits your budget. Make sure it has a powerful enough motor to whiz up all your ingredients to a fine pulp.

Making juice without a juicer

To make juice without a juicer, simply put all the ingredients into your blender and blend until liquefied. Pour the contents into a nonmetallic fine-mesh sieve set over a bowl and, using a rubber spatula or wooden spoon, gently push the juice through the sieve. Discard the solids. There is some washing up to do with this method, but probably not as much as you would need to do with a proper juicer.

Basic equipment

- *blender*
- *fine-mesh sieve*
- *large bowl*
- *rubber spatula or wooden spoon*
- *saucepan*

HOW TO DESIGN YOUR OWN DETOX PLAN

Designing a detox plan can sometimes be difficult. Use the lists on pages 10 and 11 as a guide to help you choose what fruit and vegetables you should use for different health issues.

What ingredients to buy?

Try to buy organic fruits and vegetables, as these are free of artificial fertilizers and pesticides. They also contain higher levels of some vitamins, minerals, and micronutrients, and they are much better for the environment, soil fertility—and us. Store fresh fruits and vegetables in a cool, dry place so they last longer.

Getting ready for a detox

It is important to prepare mentally and to get into a positive frame of mind before you start a detox. This will help you complete your detox successfully. Try to detox on a day when you can relax and rest as much as possible; this will benefit your whole system. Maybe have a massage or a sauna to help with the cleansing process, or just make sure you have a really good night's sleep.

Making sure you have all the ingredients you need a day ahead is vital for preparation. Also try to eat lightly the day before, avoiding meat, fish, eggs, dairy, and wheat. A light, clean diet is also useful when you have finished your detox, to slowly bring your body back to regular meals. If you are a coffee addict, you may experience a caffeine withdrawal headache on a detox day. If this happens, you can either wean yourself off coffee during the week before the detox day, or simply allow yourself one small cup of black coffee during the detox day to keep the headaches at bay.

Any detox program is greatly enhanced if you also do some light exercise, such as yoga or walking, or even breathing exercises. A detox for three consecutive days is a commitment, so try not to plan a detox when you have a lot of other activities going on at the same time. Make sure your family and close friends know you are doing it, so they can support you and not make as many demands on you.

The first day

The first day is always the hardest. Your body needs time to adapt to going without food, and you may feel a little hungry. Don't panic! The rewards are great, the hunger pangs will pass, and you will have more energy and clarity of mind after detoxing than you might have believed possible.

How to Make a Detox Smoothie

1

First, choose your leafy greens.

kale, cabbage, spinach, Swiss chard, etc.

2

Add your detox fruits and vegetables.

see lists or choose your favorite fruit

3

Add a boost.

chia seed oil, nut butter, fresh ginger, maca, vanilla, fresh mint, fresh herbs, cinnamon, raw honey

4

Add a liquid.

filtered water, coconut water, nut milk

Top Fruits and Vegetables for a Detox

The lists below are divided into various health issues to help you choose the best fruits and vegetables for that particular condition.

 ### Skin health

Suffer from acne, skin needs a boost, antiaging

apple, avocado, broccoli, carrot, celery, cucumbers, fennel, grapefruit, kale, mango, melon, onion, orange, pumpkin, spinach, strawberry

 ### Stress busting

Suffer from anxiety and stress regularly

banana, broccoli, celery, kale, lemon, lettuce, lime, orange, peach, spinach, Swiss chard, tomato, watercress

 ### Blood cleansing

Suffer from a range of ailments, including high acid levels in body

avocado, beet, broccoli, cabbage, carrot, celery, cilantro, ginger, grape, kale, lemon, lettuce, orange, peach, pear, red pepper, spinach, tomato, watermelon

 ### Better digestion

Suffer from sluggish feeling, constipation

apple, beet, blackberry, brussels sprout, cabbage, carrot, fennel, fig, flaxseed, grape, kale, lettuce, orange, papaya, parsnip, peach, prune, pumpkin, watercress

 ### Energy boosting

Suffer from slow metabolism, feeling tired

apple, apricot, banana, bell pepper, blueberry, cantaloupe, carrot, cayenne pepper, fennel, grapefruit, kale, lemon, mango, orange, parsley, parsnip, peach, pear, spinach, strawberry, sweet potatoes

The lists below are separated into different colors to help you decide what to have in your smoothie on a daily basis.

Red

cherry, radish, raspberry, red pepper, strawberry, tomato

- Contain lycopene
- May protect cells, helping in the prevention of heart disease
- Help protect the skin from sun damage
- May help to protect against certain cancers

Orange and Yellow

apricot, carrot, clementine, mango, nectarine, orange, papaya, peach, satsuma, sweet potato, tangerine

- Contain beta-carotene, which enhances your immune system
- Convert to vitamin A in the body, essential for eyesight, immune function, and skin and bone health
- Contain hesperetin, which may lower cardiovascular risk
- Contain beta-cryptoxanthin, which helps against development of rheumatoid arthritis

Purple

beet, blackberry, black currant, blueberry, fig, plum,

- Contain anthocyanidins, which provide protection against pain and inflammation
- May support healthy blood pressure
- Noted antiaging effects

Green

apple, asparagus, avocado, broccoli, brussels sprout, cabbage, celery, cucumber, kale, kiwi, lettuce, melon, mixed greens, pear, spinach, watercress, zucchini

- Contain lutein and zeaxanthin, which help protect the eyes from damage and reduce the risk of cataracts
- Contain isothiocyanates, which have strong anticancer properties

White

parsnip

- Contain allicin, which increases the body's ability to fight infections
- Strong anitimicrobial, antifungal, antiparasitic, and antiviral properties

SPICY LEMON AND LIME CLEANSER: SMOOTHIE 2

Makes about 1 cup

YOU NEED

Juice of ½ lemon • Juice of ½ lime • A pinch of cayenne pepper
A thumb-sized piece of ginger • 1 teaspoon agave nectar

Add all of the ingredients to the blender with ¾ cup of filtered water. Blend until
smooth, then pour into a sieve set over a bowl. Help the juice through by
pressing with a rubber spatula or wooden spoon.

This should be consumed every day of your detox. It is there to keep your metabolism high, boost immunity, and give your system an alkalizer each day. It can also offer some relief from the fruit and vegetable smoothies.

MB *Metabolism Boosting* B *Blood Stimulating* DC *Deep Cleansing*

METABOLISM

Your metabolism is what runs your body: boosting it can get your blood pumping and your energy levels into gear. We often become sluggish as we get older, and feel like we need to slow down. With this, our metabolism starts to slow, which leads to our burning fewer calories. So if our diet hasn't changed, this can lead to our putting on weight. Exercising regularly and getting plenty of sleep are great things to do, as is eating the right foods. This is all vital in helping you maintain and keep your metabolism at an optimal rate. Try this smoothie plan to give your metabolism the kick it might need.

Good foods to help increase metabolism

Apples and pears
These delicious fruits are high in fiber, which is great for helping you feel full. They also contain fructose, which causes the metabolic rate to increase.

Oat bran
This is a whole grain that contains nutrients and complex carbohydrates; it speeds up metabolism by stabilizing insulin levels. Oat bran keeps your energy on an even keel and helps prevent the body from storing extra fat.

Cayenne pepper
Spicy chiles like cayenne can directly boost metabolism and blood circulation. The compound capsaicin stimulates the body's pain receptors, temporarily increasing blood circulation and therefore your metabolic rate.

How many days to detox?
This is a five-day detox plan, but if you haven't detoxed before, I recommend three days for your first time.

Preparation
Shop for your ingredients two days before. Stock up on lemons, herbal teas, and green teas, which help speed up your metabolism. Make the smoothies and juices a day before to help you keep to the plan.

Schedule
There are six smoothies to consume each day. Start the morning with a nutrient-dense smoothie, break it up with the cleanser, and end with a nut milk to help prevent you from being hungry in the evening. You don't need to drink your smoothie in one go; you can happily sip each one if you prefer. I find a wide straw very helpful.

Daily plan
Repeat this schedule every day.

Smoothie 1: 8 am
Smoothie 2 (the cleanser): 11 am
  (see page 12)
Smoothie 3: 1 pm
Smoothie 4: 3 pm
Smoothie 5: 5 pm
Smoothie 6: 7:30 pm

You don't need to stick to these times, but allow two hours of no consuming before bed. Drink lots of water; I recommend 6 to 8 cups a day.

OATY NANA: SMOOTHIE 1

Makes about 1¼ cups

YOU NEED

2 tablespoons oat bran • 1 banana, peeled • ¾ cup live-culture plain yogurt
1 tablespoon coconut oil • 1 medjool date, pitted

———————

Add all of the ingredients to the blender with ⅓ to ½ cup of filtered water.
Blend until smooth.

This helps keep your blood sugar levels on an even keel.

CR *Cholesterol Reducing* **D** *Digestion Boosting* **RJ** *Rejuvenating*

KALE CARE: SMOOTHIE 3

Makes about 1¼ cups

YOU NEED

3 handfuls kale • 2 pears, cored • 1 lime, peeled • A handful of green grapes

———————

Add all of the ingredients to the blender with ⅔ cup of filtered water. Blend until smooth, then pour into a sieve set over a bowl. Help the juice through by pressing gently with a rubber spatula or wooden spoon.

This is full of vitamin K, which helps strengthen bones, prevents calcium buildup in tissues, and improves the nervous system.

BB *Blood Building* **D** *Digestion Boosting* **ME** *Mineral Enhancing*

LIME ZEST: SMOOTHIE 4

Makes about 1 cup

YOU NEED

2 pears, cored • A handful of baby spinach

5 broccoli florets • 1 lime, ½ zested, then peeled

Add all of the ingredients to the blender with ¾ cup of filtered water. Blend until smooth, then pour into a sieve set over a bowl. Help the juice through by pressing gently with a rubber spatula or wooden spoon.

This is full of flavonoids, which help to rejuvenate the skin.

A *Anti-inflammatory* **BE** *Blood Enhancing* **BPL** *Blood Pressure Lowering*

CARROT FRESH: SMOOTHIE 5

Makes about 1²⁄₃ cups

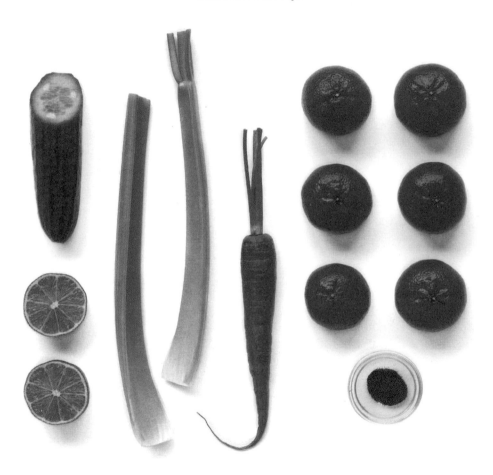

YOU NEED

1 carrot • A pinch of cayenne pepper • 6 clementines, peeled
1 lime, peeled • 2 celery stalks • ¼ cucumber

Add all of the ingredients to the blender with ⅓ to ½ cup of filtered water. Blend
until smooth, then pour into a sieve set over a bowl. Help the juice through by
pressing gently with a rubber spatula or wooden spoon.

This is good for boosting circulation and energizing the heart.

Vitamin Enhancing *Metabolism Boosting* *Anti-inflammatory*

VANILLA NUT MILK CHAI: SMOOTHIE 6

Makes about 1¼ cups

YOU NEED

2½ ounces cashew nuts • 2 drops vanilla extract • 1 tablespoon coconut oil
1 teaspoon raw cacao nibs • 2 medjool dates, pitted • 1 chai tea bag

Add all of the ingredients except for the tea bag to the blender; add 1¼ cups
of filtered water. Blend until smooth, then pour into a sieve set over a bowl.
Help the nut milk through by pressing gently with a rubber spatula or wooden
spoon. Pour the nut milk into a saucepan and add the tea bag. Warm gently
over low heat for 3 to 4 minutes.

This nut milk contains phosphorus, which provides energy and helps strengthen teeth and bones.

C Calming   H Healing   IF Infection Fighting

CLEAR SKIN

Everyone's skin battles daily with exposure to toxins from pollution, sun damage, and chemicals. These can all contribute to your skin's deterioration and lead to premature wrinkles. As our first line of defense against the environment, your skin needs to stay supple and strong. Skin problems range from eczema to psoriasis, acne to wrinkles. No one wants dry, flaky skin, and an excess of oil production can lead to outbreaks of pimples and thinning of the skin. These all need a little help from the inside.

Good foods to help with skin health

Fennel
This is a great source of vitamin C, which helps regenerate and repair cells. Supporting collagen formation, fennel contains a phytonutrient that reduces inflammation as well as properties that balance the bacteria in your gut and promote detoxification.

Apples
As well as being full of phytonutrients, apples contain enzymes that help break down carbohydrates. These help regulate blood sugar levels, which is important in skin health, as spikes in blood sugar can damage collagen.

Cucumbers
Full of minerals and B vitamins, cucumbers are fantastic for hydrating the skin, as they are 95 percent water and contain important electrolytes.

How many days to detox?
If you have never detoxed before, then you may want to start with a three-day detox. If you regularly drink green juices, have done this detox before, or eat a lot of raw food, then this detox can last five days.

Preparation
Shop for your ingredients two days before. Stock up on lemons and herbal teas. Make the smoothies and juices a day before to help you keep to the plan.

Schedule
There are six smoothies to consume each day. Start the morning with a nutrient-dense smoothie, break it up with the cleanser, and end with a nut milk to help prevent you from being hungry in the evening. You don't need to drink your smoothie in one go; you can happily sip each one if you prefer. I find a wide straw very helpful.

Daily plan
Repeat this schedule every day.

Smoothie 1: 8 am
Smoothie 2 (the cleanser): 11 am
  (see page 12)
Smoothie 3: 1 pm
Smoothie 4: 3 pm
Smoothie 5: 5 pm
Smoothie 6: 7:30 pm

You don't need to stick to these times, but allow two hours of no consuming before bed. Drink lots of water; I recommend 6 to 8 cups a day.

APPLE LUSH: SMOOTHIE 1

Makes about 1¼ cups

YOU NEED

½ green apple, cored • ½ red apple, cored • 1 celery stalk

½ yellow pepper • A handful of spinach • ½ fennel bulb

A handful of kale • ½ lemon, peeled • A thumb-sized piece of ginger • ¼ cucumber

---

Add all of the ingredients to the blender with ⅓ to ½ cup of filtered water. Blend
until smooth, then pour into a sieve set over a bowl. Help the juice through by
pressing gently with a rubber spatula or wooden spoon.

This is full of vitamins, including A, C, B-6, and especially folate (vitamin B-9), which helps your body make DNA.

BR *Blood Regulating* **A** *Anti-inflammatory* **HD** *Hydrating*

PINEAPPLE BOOST: SMOOTHIE 3

Makes about 1¼ cups

YOU NEED

1 orange, peeled • ½ fennel bulb • ¼ cup aloe vera juice
½ pineapple, peeled and chopped • 10 mint leaves • 2 handfuls spinach

---

Add all of the ingredients to the blender. Blend until smooth, then
pour into a sieve set over a bowl. Help the juice through by pressing
gently with a rubber spatula or wooden spoon.

This is high in vitamin C, which is required for collagen synthesis. Collagen is the main structural protein required for maintaining blood vessels, skin, and bones.

(A) *Anti-inflammatory* (ME) *Mineral Enhancing* (D) *Digestion Boosting*

THAI CUCUMBER: SMOOTHIE 4

Makes about 1¼ cups

YOU NEED

¼ cucumber • ½ cantaloupe, seeded and peeled

1 lemongrass stalk • 2 handfuls kale • ⅓ to ½ cup coconut water

---

Add all of the ingredients to the blender. Blend until smooth, then pour into a sieve
set over a bowl. Help the juice through by pressing gently with a rubber spatula
or wooden spoon.

This is high in vitamin A, which is important for healthy teeth, skin, bones, and mucous membranes. It also helps with eyesight.

R *Regenerating* A *Anti-inflammatory* DX *Detoxifying*

GREEN GLOW: SMOOTHIE 5

Makes about 1¼ cups

YOU NEED

3 broccoli florets • ½ fennel bulb • 1 apple, cored • ¼ cucumber • 5 sprigs cilantro

---

Add all of the ingredients to the blender with ⅓ to ½ cup of filtered water. Blend until smooth, then pour into a sieve set over a bowl. Help the juice through by pressing gently with a rubber spatula or wooden spoon.

This is full of nutrients that help fight diseases.

HD *Hydrating* **P** *Purifying* **ME** *Mineral Enhancing*

TURMERIC ALMOND MILK: SMOOTHIE 6

Makes about 1⅓ cups

YOU NEED

3½ ounces almonds • ½ teaspoon ground turmeric
2 medjool dates, pitted • A pinch of salt

Add all of the ingredients to the blender with 1¼ cups of filtered water. Blend until
smooth, then pour into a sieve set over a bowl. Help the nut milk through
by pressing gently with a rubber spatula or wooden spoon.

This is a great protein milk that enhances alkalinity. It also helps slow the rise of blood sugar and staves off hunger.

SR *Skin Repairing* **IF** *Infection Fighting* **DX** *Detoxifying*

ENERGY BOOSTER

We all know that frequent exercise has immediate effects on our mood, heart health, and skin. We also know that it can be a great boost to our energy levels. On the other hand, if we are not eating the right foods, and not fueling up on carbohydrates, exercise often leads to adverse effects on our energy. Great slow releasers of carbohydrates are vegetables and whole grains like quinoa, spelt, and brown rice. Protein is also necessary for training and recovery; it helps restore and repair muscle tissue. Eggs, legumes, nuts, and seeds all have high amounts of protein. This detox plan has been created for when you are feeling a little lackluster and need an energy boost, and to support you if are exercising regularly.

Good foods to help with energy boosting

Bananas
These are a great source of antioxidants and of healthy carbohydrates, which break down into blood sugar for fuel. Because bananas do break down so quickly, mix with a protein or healthy fat like peanut butter.

Spinach
This is great for boosting your body's iron. Iron deficiency can be a common cause of fatigue.

Grapefruit
Vitamin C (which grapefruit is full of) plays a role in helping your body form amino acids, which are precursors to chemicals that regulate your energy levels. One of the first signs of vitamin C deficiency is fatigue.

Sweet potatoes
This starchy vegetable contains slow-releasing carbohydrates that provide you with long-lasting energy. They are also full of other important energy nutrients such as vitamin C.

How many days to detox?
This is a three-day detox plan.

Preparation
Shop for your ingredients two days before. Stock up on lemons and herbal teas. Make the smoothies and juices a day before to help you keep to the plan.

Schedule
There are six smoothies to consume each day. Start the morning with a nutrient-dense smoothie, break it up with the cleanser, and end with a nut milk to help prevent you from being hungry in the evening. You don't need to drink your smoothie in one go; you can happily sip each one if you prefer. I find a wide straw very helpful.

Daily plan
Repeat this schedule every day.

Smoothie 1: 8 am
Smoothie 2 (the cleanser): 11 am
  (see page 12)
Smoothie 3: 1 pm
Smoothie 4: 3 pm
Smoothie 5: 5 pm
Smoothie 6: 7:30 pm

You don't need to stick to these times, but allow two hours of no consuming before bed. Drink lots of water; I recommend 6 to 8 cups a day.

SWEET CARBONATER: SMOOTHIE 1

Makes about 1¼ cups

YOU NEED

About ½ medium sweet potato, peeled and chopped into small chunks

2 handfuls kale • A handful of spinach

2 peaches, pitted • 2 sprigs mint • 1 lime, peeled

Add all of the ingredients to the blender with ¾ cup of filtered water. Blend until smooth, then pour into a sieve set over a bowl. Help the juice through by gently pressing with a rubber spatula or wooden spoon.

This contains high amounts of vitamin D, which plays an important role in our energy levels and moods and helps build healthy bones, heart, nerves, skin, and teeth.

E *Energizing* **ME** *Mineral Enhancing* **D** *Digestion Boosting*

BANANA BOOST: SMOOTHIE 3

Makes about 1 cup

YOU NEED
1 banana, peeled • 1 tablespoon peanut butter • 1 cup coconut water

Add all of the ingredients to the blender and blend until smooth.

This is high in potassium and vitamin B-6, which is great for strengthening your blood and preventing high blood pressure.

D *Digestion Boosting* **HD** *Hydrating* **E** *Energizing*

GRAPEFRUIT GROWER: SMOOTHIE 4

Makes about 1 cup

YOU NEED

1 medium carrot • A handful of spinach • A handful of kale
1 orange, peeled • 1 grapefruit, peeled

Add all of the ingredients to the blender with ⅓ to ½ cup of filtered water. Blend
until smooth, then pour into a sieve set over a bowl. Help the juice through by
pressing gently with a rubber spatula or wooden spoon.

This helps curb hunger. It is high in both vitamin C and beta-carotene.

Ⓥ *Vitamin Enhancing* Ⓐ *Alkalizing* ⓇⒻ *Refreshing*

REFRESHING BEET: SMOOTHIE 5

Makes about 1¼ cups

YOU NEED

3 beets • A handful of baby spinach • 2 handfuls blueberries • ¼ cucumber

Add all of the ingredients to the blender with ⅔ cup of filtered water. Blend until smooth, then pour into a sieve set over a bowl. Help the juice through by pressing gently with a rubber spatula or wooden spoon.

This helps boost your stamina and makes muscles work
more efficiently, reducing blood pressure.

E *Energizing* **BB** *Blood Building* **S** *Strengthening*

SPICED SWEET POTATO MILK: SMOOTHIE 6

Makes about 1¼ cups

YOU NEED

2½ ounces almonds • ½ medium sweet potato, peeled and chopped
½ teaspoon ground cinnamon • A pinch of ground cloves
A thumb-sized piece of ginger • 2 medjool dates, pitted
1 teaspoon honey • A pinch of salt

Add all of the ingredients to the blender with 1¼ cups of filtered water. Blend until smooth, then pour into a sieve set over a bowl. Help the nut milk through by pressing gently with a rubber spatula or wooden spoon. Warm this nut milk up, if you prefer, by slowly heating it in a saucepan for 3 to 4 minutes.

This helps regulate your blood sugar levels and keep hunger at bay.

RJ *Rejuvenating* **BPL** *Blood Pressure* **C** *Calming*

DIGESTION

A healthy gut (otherwise known as your second brain) is an important part of your body to keep healthy. Undigested material needs to continue moving through the large intestine, where water is absorbed and fecal matter is formed. (If you are a healthy eater, getting rid of this matter will be a routine part of your day, but if your diet is high in animal products and processed foods, it might be a painful part of your week!) The major detoxification organ is the large intestine, and it is vital that you keep this clean and toned so it can absorb nutrients properly. Eating a mostly plant-based, whole-food diet and drinking green smoothies will keep nasty toxins away and repair damage to cell tissue caused by free radicals.

Good foods to help with digestion

Papayas
Rich in protein-digesting enzymes, which help break down the dietary proteins in the stomach and intestines, papayas regulate the digestive system and support peristalsis, promoting regular bowel movements.

Carrots
A great food to support the liver, carrots encourage bile production, which helps with constipation by binding bile acids, encouraging peristalsis and the movement of waste through the intestine.

Apples
These contain a natural laxative called sorbitol, which holds on to water as it makes its way through the gut, drawing it into the large intestine. This promotes regular bowel movements. Sorbitol can also be found in prunes, peaches, and pears.

How many days to detox?
This is a five-day detox plan, but if you haven't detoxed before, I recommend three days for your first time.

Preparation
Shop for your ingredients two days before. Stock up on lemons and herbal teas, particularly mint, nettle, and fennel, as these help with digestion. Make the smoothies and juices a day before to help you keep to the plan.

Schedule
There are six smoothies to consume each day. Start the morning with a nutrient-dense smoothie, break it up with the cleanser, and end with a nut milk to help prevent you from being hungry in the evening. You don't need to drink your smoothie in one go; you can happily sip each one if you prefer. I find a wide straw very helpful.

Daily plan
Repeat this schedule every day.

Smoothie 1: 8 am
Smoothie 2 (the cleanser): 11 am
  (see page 12)
Smoothie 3: 1 pm
Smoothie 4: 3 pm
Smoothie 5: 5 pm
Smoothie 6: 7:30 pm

You don't need to stick to these times, but allow two hours of no consuming before bed. Drink lots of water; I recommend 6 to 8 cups a day.

DIGESTIVO: SMOOTHIE 1

Makes about 1¼ cups

YOU NEED

1 papaya, peeled and seeded • 2 handfuls kale

1 green apple, cored • 1 red apple, cored • 1 carrot

Add all of the ingredients to the blender with ¾ cup of filtered water. Blend until smooth, then pour into a sieve set over a bowl. Help the juice through by pressing gently with a rubber spatula or wooden spoon.

This is great at breaking down proteins, aiding digestion.

D *Digestion Boosting* **LC** *Liver Cleansing* **HD** *Hydrating*

PEACHY CARROTS: SMOOTHIE 3

Makes about 1¼ cups

YOU NEED
2 peaches, pitted • A handful of spinach • 2 medium carrots • ¼ cucumber

Add all of the ingredients to the blender with ¾ cup of filtered water. Blend until smooth, then pour into a sieve set over a bowl. Help the juice through by pressing gently with a rubber spatula or wooden spoon.

Full of vitamins and minerals as well as antioxidants
and fiber, this is a great all-rounder.

LC *Liver Cleansing* **CR** *Cholesterol Reducing* **V** *Vitamin Enhancing*

BERRY BUZZ: SMOOTHIE 4

Makes about 1¼ cups

YOU NEED

A handful of kale • ½ romaine lettuce • 10 strawberries, hulled
1 kiwi fruit, peeled • 1 lime, peeled

Add all of the ingredients to the blender with ⅔ cup of filtered water. Blend until smooth, then pour into a sieve set over a bowl. Help the juice through by pressing gently with a rubber spatula or wooden spoon.

A rich source of vitamin C and fiber, this also helps lower cholesterol.

 Strengthening  Brain Boosting  Vitamin Enhancing

REFLAX: SMOOTHIE 5

Makes about 1 cup

YOU NEED

1 tablespoon flaxseed oil • 2 celery stalks • 5 sprigs parsley
½ fennel bulb • A handful of green grapes

Add all of the ingredients to the blender with ⅔ cup of filtered water. Blend until smooth, then pour into a sieve set over a bowl. Help the juice through by pressing gently with a rubber spatula or wooden spoon.

This is high in antioxidants, which help prevent disease.

D *Digestion Boosting* **DX** *Detoxifying* **A** *Anti-inflammatory*

FENNEL SPICED NUT MILK: SMOOTHIE 6

Makes about 1¼ cups

YOU NEED

1 ounce almonds • 1 ounce cashew nuts • 1 ounce pistachio nuts
2 medjool dates, pitted • 1 teaspoon fennel seeds • 2 cardamom pods
½ teaspoon ground cinnamon

Add the almonds, cashew nuts, pistachio nuts, and dates to the blender with 1¼ cups
of filtered water. Blend until smooth, then pour into a sieve set over a bowl. Help
the nut milk through by pressing gently with a rubber spatula or wooden spoon.
Pour into a saucepan; add the fennel seeds, cardamom pods, and cinnamon;
and warm gently over low heat for 3 to 4 minutes. Sieve again, then serve.

This is a great nut milk to increase your iron intake as well as reduce indigestion.

C *Calming* **BB** *Blood Building* **I** *Immune Boosting*

STRESS BUSTER

When we suffer from stress, the stress hormones adrenaline and cortisol are released from our adrenal glands, which are found at the top of our kidneys. This leads to a rise in blood sugar, flexing of muscles, shallow breathing, higher blood pressure, and rapid heart rate, otherwise known as the fight-or-flight response, which can lead to diabetes, weight gain, and digestive problems. Luckily, we can reduce stress with diet and lifestyle changes. Eating regularly and sleeping for eight hours can help your body relax. Eating complex carbohydrates while avoiding both sugars and snacking can help. Replacing stimulants like alcohol and caffeine with nutrient-dense fuel like green juices can also significantly reduce these symptoms.

Good foods to combat stress

Celery
Phthalides, found in the phytonutrients in celery, have a sedative effect, which can help reduce the stress hormones and relax the arterial muscle walls, which increases blood flow. Celery is also an excellent source of vitamins K, C, and B-6, potassium, folate, and fiber.

Bananas
Vitamin B-6 deficiency has been said to decrease production of serotonin, which is one of the key chemicals in your body to regulate your mood; by eating bananas daily, you can keep your serotonin levels up, as well as your potassium levels.

Swiss chard
Stress can cause feelings of anxiety and irritability, which may cause a magnesium deficiency in your body. Swiss chard increases your intake of magnesium, which can help reduce anxiety.

How many days to detox?
This is a five-day detox plan, but if you haven't detoxed before, I recommend three days for your first time.

Preparation
Shop for your ingredients two days before. Stock up on lemons and herbal teas. Make the smoothies and juices a day before to help you keep to the plan.

Schedule
There are six smoothies to consume each day. Start the morning with a nutrient-dense smoothie, break it up with the cleanser, and end with a nut milk to help prevent you from being hungry in the evening. You don't need to drink your smoothie in one go; you can happily sip each one if you prefer. I find a wide straw very helpful.

Daily plan
Repeat this schedule every day.

Smoothie 1: 8 am
Smoothie 2 (the cleanser): 11 am
  (see page 12)
Smoothie 3: 1 pm
Smoothie 4: 3 pm
Smoothie 5: 5 pm
Smoothie 6: 7:30 pm

You don't need to stick to these times, but allow two hours of no consuming before bed. Drink lots of water; I recommend 6 to 8 cups a day.

BANANA SPICE: SMOOTHIE 1

Makes about 1 cup

YOU NEED

1 banana, peeled • ¾ cup live-culture plain yogurt • 1 tablespoon almond butter
1 medjool date, pitted • ½ teaspoon ground cinnamon

Add all of the ingredients to the blender with ¼ cup of filtered water. Blend until smooth, then pour into a sieve set over a bowl. Help the juice through by gently pressing with a rubber spatula or wooden spoon.

This is high in tryptophan, which converts in the body to serotonin, which in turn helps improve your mood.

RG *Regulating* **V** *Vitamin Enhancing* **MBB** *Muscle & Bone Building*

BUNCH OF CELERY: SMOOTHIE 3

Makes about 1¼ cups

YOU NEED

2 celery stalks • ½ cucumber

2 handfuls kale • 1 apple, cored • ½ lemon, peeled • 1 teaspoon honey

---

Add all of the ingredients to the blender with ⅔ cup of filtered water. Blend until smooth, then pour into a sieve set over a bowl. Help the juice through by pressing gently with a rubber spatula or wooden spoon.

This is great as a postworkout drink, as it replaces
electrolytes and rehydrates the body.

SS *Stress Reducing* **BE** *Blood Enhancing* **V** *Vitamin Enhancing*

GREEN ALBA: SMOOTHIE 4

Makes about 1 cup

YOU NEED

4 Swiss chard leaves, including stems • 2 handfuls kale
2 celery stalks • 1 kiwi fruit, peeled • 1 cup coconut water

Add all of the ingredients to the blender. Blend until smooth, then pour
into a sieve set over a bowl. Help the juice through by pressing gently with
a rubber spatula or wooden spoon.

This is a nutrient-rich drink that helps regulate blood sugar levels.

HD *Hydrating*   **SS** *Stress Reducing*   **MB** *Metabolism Boosting*

PARSLEY PINEAPPLE: SMOOTHIE 5

Makes about 1²⁄₃ cups

YOU NEED

⅓ pineapple, peeled and cut into chunks • 2 celery stalks

2 handfuls spinach • A few sprigs of parsley

Add all of the ingredients to the blender with ¼ cup of filtered water. Blend until smooth, then pour into a sieve set over a bowl. Help the juice through by pressing gently with a rubber spatula or wooden spoon.

This is full of antioxidants, increasing oxygen in the blood.

DR *Diuretic* **RJ** *Rejuvenating* **RV** *Revitalizing*

MANGO NUT MILK: SMOOTHIE 6

Makes about 1½ cups

YOU NEED

2½ ounces cashew nuts • 1 mango, peeled, pitted, and cut into chunks
1 tablespoon chia seed oil

Add all of the ingredients to the blender with 1¼ cups of filtered water. Blend until smooth, then pour into a sieve set over a bowl. Help the nut milk through by pressing gently with a rubber spatula or wooden spoon. If you feel it is a little thick to drink, try adding more water, or get yourself a spoon.

This nut milk helps alkalize the body and clear the skin.

C *Calming* **V** *Vitamin Enhancing* **I** *Immune Boosting*

PURIFYING

Sometimes we feel that our body is running on empty, that it is sluggish in movement or perhaps in need of recharging. We usually think of taking a vacation to help us with this, but if that isn't an option, this purifying detox is a good alternative.

To keep a healthy body, it is good to get rid of excessive waste products and generally give ourselves a flush—and to expose ourselves to many healthy nutrients. Thankfully, smoothies are a good way to do this. This purifying detox plan will give anyone's liver a great boost.

Good foods to help purify your body

Ginger
This spice contains a substance called gingerol, which is an antioxidant and anti-inflammatory.

Avocados
High in fiber and good fat, as well as many minerals and vitamins, avocado also has strong anti-inflammatory properties.

Broccoli
A rich source of essential nutrients, broccoli has many health benefits. It contains anticancer and antioxidant compounds that help the liver to detoxify and clean blood.

Cilantro
This herb is great at detoxifying the body of heavy metals.

How many days to detox?
This is a five-day detox plan, but if you haven't detoxed before, I recommend three days for your first time.

Preparation
Shop for your ingredients two days before. Stock up on lemons and herbal teas. Drink ginger tea throughout the day: 1 tablespoon grated ginger, boiled water, honey, and a squeeze of lemon. Garlic is a natural antibiotic, so take it as a supplement. Make the smoothies and juices a day before to help you keep to the plan.

Schedule
There are six smoothies to consume each day. Start the morning with a nutrient-dense smoothie, break it up with the cleanser, and end with a nut milk to help prevent you from being hungry in the evening. You don't need to drink your smoothie in one go; you can happily sip each one if you prefer. I find a wide straw very helpful.

Daily plan
Repeat this schedule every day.

Smoothie 1: 8 am
Smoothie 2 (the cleanser): 11 am
  (see page 12)
Smoothie 3: 1 pm
Smoothie 4: 3 pm
Smoothie 5: 5 pm
Smoothie 6: 7:30 pm

You don't need to stick to these times, but allow two hours of no consuming before bed. Drink lots of water; I recommend 6 to 8 cups a day.

VELVET GREEN: SMOOTHIE 1

Makes about 1¼ cups

YOU NEED

1 apple, peeled and cored • 1 fennel bulb • ¼ cucumber

1 avocado, peeled and pitted • A small handful of green grapes

---

Add all of the ingredients to the blender with ⅓ to ½ cup of filtered water.
Blend until smooth. If you feel it is a little thick, just add more water.

High in iron, this contains nutrients that aid digestion.

ME *Mineral Enhancing*   **A** *Anti-inflammatory*   **DR** *Diuretic*

SPROUTING SUCCESS: SMOOTHIE 3

Makes about 1 cup

YOU NEED

2 handfuls kale • A few sprigs of parsley • 1 kiwi fruit, peeled

1 lime, peeled • 4 broccoli florets

A handful of green grapes • ½ teaspoon spirulina powder

Add all of the ingredients to the blender with ¾ cup of filtered water.
Blend until smooth, then pour into a sieve set over a bowl. Help the juice
through by pressing gently with a rubber spatula or wooden spoon.

This is high in vitamin C and keeps your liver healthy.

BP *Blood Purifying* **MO** *Mood Enhancing* **IF** *Infection Fighting*

SWEET ROOTS: SMOOTHIE 4

Makes about 1¼ cups

YOU NEED

1 carrot • 1 parsnip • 1 medium potato • 1 lemongrass stalk • 1 apple, cored
1 lime, peeled • 10 cilantro sprigs • 1 tablespoon chia seed oil

Add all of the ingredients to the blender with ¾ cup of filtered water. Blend until smooth, then pour into a sieve set over a bowl. Help the juice through by pressing gently with a rubber spatula or wooden spoon. If you feel it is a little thick, just add a little more water.

This is high in folate and potassium, which are great for cardiovascular health.

LC *Liver Cleansing* **D** *Digestion Boosting* **AO** *Antioxidant*

MELON MADNESS: SMOOTHIE 5

Makes about 1 cup

YOU NEED

5 broccoli florets • ¼ small watermelon, peeled and seeded
½ cantaloupe, peeled and seeded • A thumb-sized piece of ginger

---

Add all of the ingredients to the blender. Blend until smooth, then
pour into a sieve set over a bowl. Help the juice through by pressing
gently with a rubber spatula or wooden spoon.

This is great at reducing inflammation and at
keeping your skin healthy with vitamin A.

BP *Blood Purifying* **HD** *Hydrating* **MV** *Mineral & Vitamin Enhancing*

GINGER MILK NOG: SMOOTHIE 6

Makes about 1¼ cups

YOU NEED

3½ ounces almonds • A thumb-sized piece of ginger • 1 teaspoon honey

Add all of the ingredients to the blender with 1¼ cups of filtered water. Blend until
smooth, then pour into a sieve set over a bowl. Help the nut milk through
by pressing gently with a rubber spatula or wooden spoon.

This nut milk naturally boosts your immune system.

C *Calming* **H** *Healing* **MBB** *Muscle & Bone Building*

PROBIOTIC

What you eat and drink has so much to do with your overall health. Where does good health start? In your gut! Our gut needs good bacteria to help fight infection. Not only do good bacteria defend our bodies, they also nourish us by producing vitamins B-1, B-2, B-5, B-6, and K, and essential fatty acids, antioxidants, and amino acids. To keep your gut healthy, you need to feed it with lots of vitamins and minerals. Fresh green vegetables have many beneficial effects, including helping support good bacteria in the gut.

Good foods to help your stomach

Flaxseeds
When these are digested, your intestinal bacteria activate phytoestrogens called lignans. These are believed to have anticancer, anti-inflammatory, and cholesterol-lowering properties. Add flaxseed oil to a finished juice or smoothie.

Yogurt
Live-culture plain yogurt—and even more so, homemade yogurt—is high in probiotics. Check the label, as some brands are filled with high-fructose corn syrup and artificial sweeteners. Goat's milk yogurt is particularly high in probiotics.

Spirulina
This superfood is a type of seaweed, which when taken increases the amounts of lactobacillus and bifidobacteria in the digestive tract. As an added bonus, it also gives you lots of energy.

How many days to detox?
This is a five-day detox plan, but if you haven't detoxed before, I recommend three days for your first time.

Preparation
Shop for your ingredients two days before. Stock up on lemons and herbal teas. Drink kombucha tea, a form of fermented tea, if you can find it. This tea contains lots of healthy gut bacteria. Make the smoothies and juices a day before to help you keep to the plan.

Schedule
There are six smoothies to consume each day. Start the morning with a nutrient-dense smoothie, break it up with the cleanser, and end with a nut milk to help prevent you from being hungry in the evening. You don't need to drink your smoothie in one go; you can happily sip each one if you prefer. I find a wide straw very helpful.

Daily plan
Repeat this schedule every day.

Smoothie 1: 8 am
Smoothie 2 (the cleanser): 11 am
  (see page 12)
Smoothie 3: 1 pm
Smoothie 4: 3 pm
Smoothie 5: 5 pm
Smoothie 6: 7:30 pm

You don't need to stick to these times, but allow two hours of no consuming before bed. Drink lots of water; I recommend 6 to 8 cups a day.

MORNING YOGURT: SMOOTHIE 1

Makes about 1⅔ cups

YOU NEED

¾ cup live-culture plain yogurt • 2 handfuls blueberries • 8 strawberries, hulled

⅓ to ½ cup almond milk • 1 tablespoon oat bran • 1 tablespoon flaxseed oil

————

Add all of the ingredients to the blender and blend until smooth.

This is a good source of vitamin K, which
helps in strengthening bones and building blood.

 Soothing  Healing  Digestion Boosting

KLEAN KALE: SMOOTHIE 3

Makes about 1½ cups

YOU NEED

½ romaine lettuce • ⅓ cucumber • 2 handfuls blueberries
2 handfuls kale • 1 apple, cored

Add all of the ingredients to the blender with ⅓ to ½ cup of filtered water. Blend
until smooth, then pour into a sieve set over a bowl. Help the juice through by
pressing gently with a rubber spatula or wooden spoon.

Full of iron, vitamin C, and omega-3 and omega-6 fatty acids, this is good for boosting your skin health and strengthening your immune system.

P *Purifying*   **IF** *Infection Fighting*   **BB** *Blood Building*

TROPICAL TASTE: SMOOTHIE 4

Makes about 1 cup

YOU NEED

1 banana, peeled • ⅓ pineapple, peeled and cut into chunks
2 handfuls spinach • ⅔ cup live-culture plain yogurt

Add all of the ingredients to the blender and blend until smooth.

Full of lactobacteria and calcium, this helps protect the colon.

HD *Hydrating* BE *Blood Enhancing* BF *Bacteria Fighting*

SPIRULINA SMILE: SMOOTHIE 5

Makes about 1 cup

YOU NEED

1 pink grapefruit, peeled • 2 handfuls kale

6 large asparagus spears • 2 celery stalks • 1 teaspoon spirulina powder

Add all of the ingredients to the blender with ⅓ to ½ cup of filtered water. Blend until smooth, then pour into a sieve set over a bowl. Help the juice through by pressing gently with a rubber spatula or wooden spoon.

This is a great source of protein and essential nutrients, including a high percentage of your recommended dietary allowance of iron.

BB *Blood Building* **PE** *Protein Enriching* **AZ** *Alkalizing*

GREEN LASSI: SMOOTHIE 6

Makes about 1¼ cups

YOU NEED

2½ ounces pistachio nuts • ¾ cup live-culture plain yogurt
A thumb-sized piece of ginger • 1 medjool date, pitted • A pinch of black pepper

---

Add all of the ingredients to the blender with ⅓ to ½ cup of filtered water. Blend
until smooth, then pour into a sieve set over a bowl. Help the smoothie through by
pressing smoothie gently with a rubber spatula or wooden spoon.

This is a great smoothie to aid digestion and soothe the stomach.

C *Calming* **CR** *Cholesterol Reducing* **I** *Immune Boosting*

ALKALIZING

The pH of your blood indicates how acid or alkaline your system is. Having a low pH can mean that your body is in an acidic state, which can affect your health at a cellular level, encouraging fatigue, osteoporosis, candida, loss of muscle, kidney stones, and an increase in free radicals. The great news is that eating and drinking alkaline foods and juices is the easiest, most efficient way to replenish your cells with alkaline minerals, optimizing your well-being. Alkaline-forming foods are vegetables like lettuce, spinach, and kale. Stick to the theory that the greener they are, the more alkaline they are. Fresh fruits are good, too, and grains like quinoa, amaranth, millet, and teff are also good to include in your diet.

Good foods to encourage alkalinity

Root vegetables
As well as being rich in minerals, any root vegetable, including beets, radishes, parsnips, and carrots, are good for alkalinity.

Red peppers
Containing essential enzymes for endocrine function, red peppers are one of the best foods for alkalizing. They are also known for their antibacterial properties and rich supply of vitamin A, and are helpful in fighting off the free radicals that lead to stress and illness.

Lemons
You may think of these yellow fruits as acidic, but they are not. They are the most alkalizing food of all. Naturally disinfectant, they can heal wounds while providing potent and immediate relief for hyperacidity, heartburn, and virus-related conditions like coughs, colds, and flu. Lemons also energize the liver and promote detoxification.

How many days to detox?
This is a five-day detox plan, but if you haven't detoxed before, I recommend three days for your first time.

Preparation
Shop for your ingredients two days before. Stock up on lemons and herbal teas. Make the smoothies and juices a day before to help you keep to the plan.

Schedule
There are six smoothies to consume each day. Start the morning with a nutrient-dense smoothie, break it up with the cleanser, and end with a nut milk to help prevent you from being hungry in the evening. You don't need to drink your smoothie in one go; you can happily sip each one if you prefer. I find a wide straw very helpful.

Daily plan
Repeat this schedule every day.

Smoothie 1: 8 am
Smoothie 2 (the cleanser): 11 am
  (see page 12)
Smoothie 3: 1 pm
Smoothie 4: 3 pm
Smoothie 5: 5 pm
Smoothie 6: 7:30 pm

You don't need to stick to these times, but allow two hours of no consuming before bed. Drink lots of water; I recommend 6 to 8 cups a day.

GREEN IN LINE: SMOOTHIE 1

Makes about 1¼ cups

YOU NEED

2 handfuls kale • A handful of baby spinach

¼ cucumber • A handful of green grapes • 1 kiwi fruit, peeled

Add all of the ingredients to the blender with ⅓ to ½ cup of filtered water. Blend
until smooth, then pour into a sieve set over a bowl. Help the juice through by
pressing gently with a rubber spatula or wooden spoon.

High in vitamin C, this is a great immune-boosting smoothie.

LC *Liver Cleansing* **ME** *Mineral Enhancing* **MO** *Mood Enhancing*

MORNING FRESH: SMOOTHIE 3

Makes about 1¼ cups

YOU NEED

½ romaine lettuce • 1 lemon, peeled • ½ green cabbage

1 orange, peeled • 10 mint leaves

Add all of the ingredients to the blender with ⅓ to ½ cup of filtered water. Blend until smooth, then pour into a sieve set over a bowl. Help the juice through by pressing gently with a rubber spatula or wooden spoon.

Vitamin C, folate, and potassium are in this smoothie to keep your blood sugar level.

AZ *Alkalizing* D *Digestion Boosting* V *Vitamin Enhancing*

PURPLE SUNSHINE: SMOOTHIE 4

Makes about 1½ cups

YOU NEED
¼ red cabbage • 2 celery stalks
4 plums, pitted • A large handful of blackberries

Add all of the ingredients to the blender with ⅓ to ½ cup of filtered water. Blend until smooth, then pour into a sieve set over a bowl. Help the juice through by pressing gently with a rubber spatula or wooden spoon.

This is full of powerful vitamins to keep your immune system healthy.

LC *Liver Cleansing* **DC** *Deep Cleansing* **DX** *Detoxifying*

ENERGY ROOT PEPPER: SMOOTHIE 5

Makes about 1 cup

YOU NEED

2 beets • 1 red pepper, seeded • 2 handfuls kale
1 apple, cored • 1 teaspoon barley grass juice powder

Add all of the ingredients to the blender with ¾ cup of filtered water. Blend until smooth, then pour into a sieve set over a bowl. Help the juice through by pressing gently with a rubber spatula or wooden spoon.

This is bursting with vitamins A, C, and K to support
your immune function and reduce inflammation.

A Anti-inflammatory CL Cleansing V Vitamin Enhancing

BRAZILIAN BEDTIME: SMOOTHIE 6

Makes about 1¼ cups

YOU NEED

3½ ounces Brazil nuts • 5 medjool dates, pitted • A pinch of salt

2 drops vanilla extract

Add all of the ingredients to the blender with 1¼ cups of filtered water. Blend
until smooth, then pour into a sieve set over a bowl. Help the nut milk through
by pressing gently with a rubber spatula or wooden spoon.

This nut milk has selenium, which is an essential trace mineral for immune and thyroid function.

ME *Mineral Enhancing* C *Calming* AO *Antioxidant*

SUMMER BOOSTER

This detox is an all-rounder, and doesn't concentrate on just one part of the body. If you are wanting to feel refreshed and revitalized and ready to get out there in the sunshine, this plan will give you the boost you need. Perhaps you are feeling a little tired, can't bear the thought of wearing a bikini, your skin is in need of a shine, or you have an urge to feel healthy. This plan will give you confidence, help you to feel better from within, and give a boost to your skin.

Good foods to give you a nutrient boost

Kale
This cruciferous vegetable is king when it comes to fiber. Helping you keep full for a good amount of time, it also contains antioxidants, is high in omega-3s, and even has anti-inflammatory qualities.

Raspberries
These lovely, sweet red fruits are great in smoothies, and they're still just as nutrient rich when frozen. They contain high levels of vitamins and minerals, such as potassium, calcium, and folate, that help maintain good blood pressure and promote bone growth.

Cantaloupe
Rich in vitamin C and potassium, the cantaloupe is a great, juicy fruit with many benefits for a healthy diet.

How many days to detox?
This is a five-day detox plan, but if you haven't detoxed before, I recommend three days for your first time.

Preparation
Shop for your ingredients two days before. Stock up on lemons and herbal teas. Make the smoothies and juices a day before to help you keep to the plan.

Schedule
There are six smoothies to consume each day. Start the morning with a nutrient-dense smoothie, break it up with the cleanser, and end with a nut milk to help prevent you from being hungry in the evening. You don't need to drink your smoothie in one go; you can happily sip each one if you prefer. I find a wide straw very helpful.

Daily plan
Repeat this schedule every day.

Smoothie 1: 8 am
Smoothie 2 (the cleanser): 11 am
  (see page 12)
Smoothie 3: 1 pm
Smoothie 4: 3 pm
Smoothie 5: 5 pm
Smoothie 6: 7:30 pm

You don't need to stick to these times, but allow two hours of no consuming before bed. Drink lots of water; I recommend 6 to 8 cups a day.

KALE ROOT: SMOOTHIE 1

Makes about 1¼ cups

YOU NEED
2 handfuls kale • 2 small beets
1 orange, peeled • A few sprigs of parsley • 2 celery stalks
½ lemon, peeled • 1 tablespoon flaxseed oil

Add all of the ingredients to the blender with ¾ cup of filtered water. Blend until smooth, then pour into a sieve set over a bowl. Help the juice through by pressing gently with a rubber spatula or wooden spoon.

This is high in calcium, which is good for your bones.

A *Anti-inflammatory* **AO** *Antioxidant* **D** *Digestion Boosting*

SPICED BERRIES: SMOOTHIE 3

Makes about 1¼ cups

YOU NEED

2 handfuls watercress • 2 large handfuls red grapes
2 handfuls raspberries • A thumb-sized piece of ginger

Add all of the ingredients to the blender with ¾ cup of filtered water. Blend until smooth, then pour into a sieve set over a bowl. Help the juice through by pressing gently with a rubber spatula or wooden spoon.

Highly nutritious, this is full of vitamins C and E, beta-carotene, folate, and calcium.

BB *Blood Building* **MV** *Mineral & Vitamin Enhancing* **D** *Digestion Boosting*

SUMMER MINT: SMOOTHIE 4

Makes about 1¼ cups

YOU NEED

¼ cucumber • ½ cantaloupe, peeled and seeded
2 handfuls strawberries, hulled • 5 mint leaves

Add all of the ingredients to the blender with ¼ cup of filtered water. Blend until smooth, then pour into a sieve set over a bowl. Help the juice through by pressing gently with a rubber spatula or wooden spoon.

This is a well-rounded smoothie good for a healthy immune system.

V *Vitamin Enhancing* **HD** *Hydrating* **RJ** *Rejuvenating*

CALM COMPLEXION: SMOOTHIE 5

Makes about 1²/₃ cups

YOU NEED

1 apple, peeled and cored • 2 handfuls kale

½ large avocado, peeled and seeded • ¼ cucumber

Add all of the ingredients to the blender with ¾ cup of filtered water and blend until smooth. Avocado makes it quite thick; if you want to thin it, try adding a little more water. Otherwise, try consuming with a spoon.

This is full of healthy monounsaturated
fats essential for plump, youthful skin.

SR *Skin Repairing* A *Anti-inflammatory* P *Purifying*

SLEEPY SPICE: SMOOTHIE 6

Makes about 1¼ cups

YOU NEED

2½ ounces almonds • A pinch of saffron threads

A pinch of ground cardamom, or 2 cardamom pods, seeded and ground

2 medjool dates, pitted

Add all of the ingredients to the blender with 1¼ cups of filtered water. Blend
until smooth, then pour into a sieve set over a bowl. Help the nut milk through
by pressing gently with a rubber spatula or wooden spoon.

This nut milk will lift your mood, support your eyesight, and improve your memory.

C *Calming* **H** *Healing* **BF** *Bacteria Fighting*

IMMUNITY BOOSTING

A good intake of nutrients is important for your immune system. Sometimes after you have a cold or go down with an infection, it takes a while to come back to feeling normal again. Try this detox to kickstart your immune system and give you what you need to feel yourself again.

Good foods to help boost your immune system

Açai berries
Commonly bought in dried form, the açai berry is very dark in color, which signifies that it is high in antioxidants; studies have suggested these help you maintain immune-system health as you age.

Watermelon
This colorful melon is refreshing and hydrating and contains powerful antioxidants. Glutathione is found in the red pulpy flesh near the rind; it helps fight infection and strengthen your immune system.

Cabbage
Cabbage is high in amino acids, and is believed to reduce inflammation. It is also an excellent source of vitamin C and of vitamin K. Vitamin K plays an important role in helping the body fight invaders, strengthening your immune system.

How many days to detox?
This is a five-day detox plan, but if you haven't detoxed before, I recommend three days for your first time.

Preparation
Shop for your ingredients two days before. Stock up on lemons and herbal teas. Make the smoothies and juices a day before to help you keep to the plan.

Schedule
There are six smoothies to consume each day. Start the morning with a nutrient-dense smoothie, break it up with the cleanser, and end with a nut milk to help prevent you from being hungry in the evening. You don't need to drink your smoothie in one go; you can happily sip each one if you prefer. I find a wide straw very helpful.

Daily plan
Repeat this schedule every day.

Smoothie 1: 8 am
Smoothie 2 (the cleanser): 11 am
  (see page 12)
Smoothie 3: 1 pm
Smoothie 4: 3 pm
Smoothie 5: 5 pm
Smoothie 6: 7:30 pm

You don't need to stick to these times, but allow two hours of no consuming before bed. Drink lots of water; I recommend 6 to 8 cups a day.

COCO MELON: SMOOTHIE 1

Makes about 1¼ cups

YOU NEED

⅓ to ½ cup almond milk • ¼ small watermelon, peeled and seeded

3½ ounces raw coconut • ⅓ to ½ cup live-culture plain yogurt • 1 teaspoon honey

———

Add all of the ingredients to the blender and blend until smooth, then pour
into a sieve set over a bowl. Help the juice through by pressing gently
with a rubber spatula or wooden spoon.

This is an excellent smoothie for killing harmful bacteria and viruses.

HD *Hydrating* BE *Blood Enhancing* RJ *Rejuvenating*

SAVOY BERRY: SMOOTHIE 3

Makes about 1¼ cups

YOU NEED

10 strawberries, hulled • ¼ Savoy cabbage

1 lime, peeled • A large sprig of mint

Add all of the ingredients to the blender with ¾ cup of filtered water. Blend until smooth, then pour into a sieve set over a bowl. Help the juice through by pressing gently with a rubber spatula or wooden spoon.

This is full of potent antioxidants and vitamins A, C, E, and K.

H *Healing* **I** *Immune Boosting* **IF** *Infection Fighting*

RED VEG: SMOOTHIE 4

Makes about 1¼ cups

YOU NEED

¼ cucumber • 2 small carrots • 1 celery stalk • ¼ red cabbage

1 lemon, peeled • A thumb-sized piece of ginger • A small bunch of red grapes

---

Add all of the ingredients to the blender with ¾ cup of filtered water. Blend until
smooth, then pour into a sieve set over a bowl. Help the juice through by pressing
gently with a rubber spatula or wooden spoon.

This is full of vitamin A, which helps eyesight.

MB *Metabolism Boosting*   **D** *Digestion Boosting*   **BF** *Bacteria Fighting*

AÇAI WATER: SMOOTHIE 5

Makes about 1¼ cups

YOU NEED

¼ watermelon, peeled and seeded • ½ cucumber

Several sprigs of cilantro • 1 teaspoon açai powder

Add all of the ingredients to the blender with ⅓ to ½ cup of filtered water. Blend until smooth, then pour into a sieve set over a bowl. Help the juice through by pressing gently with a rubber spatula or wooden spoon.

Full of essential fatty acids, this will set you on a path of good health.

HD *Hydrating* **V** *Vitamin Enhancing* **B** *Blood Stimulating*

CHOC B NUT: SMOOTHIE 6

Makes about 1¼ cups

YOU NEED

2½ ounces Brazil nuts • 1 tablespoon coconut oil
1 medjool date, pitted • 1 teaspoon raw cacoa nibs

Add all of the ingredients to the blender with 1¼ cups of filtered water. Blend until smooth, then pour into a sieve set over a bowl. Help the nut milk through by pressing gently with a rubber spatula or wooden spoon.

This is full of magnesium, which helps to relax muscles, improves peristalsis in the bowels, and relaxes the heart and cardiovascular system.

BR *Blood Regulating* **AO** *Antioxidant* **A** *Anti-inflammatory*

WEIGHT LOSS DETOX

If you feel that you have been overeating and perhaps not exercising as much as you would like to, then try this detox to jump-start losing a few pounds. Consuming too many fatty foods and increasing your blood sugar level can cause cravings, irritability, and mood swings. You want to feel fuller on fewer calories, so try these tips:

- *Get regular exercise, which improves your mood.*
- *Keep hydrated by drinking 6 to 8 glasses of water a day.*
- *Introduce a juice as a snack to your daily routine.*

Good foods to help keep cravings at bay

Avocados
These are great at keeping your blood sugar level. They can't be juiced, but are great in shakes and smoothies. Being quite high in calories, they are full of good fats, which the body will use up during the day.

Grapefruit
These are great at suppressing hunger, due to the phytochemicals found in them. They are full of vitamin C, and can stimulate your metabolism to burn fat.

Broccoli
Being low in calories and sugar, this vegetable is a great one to add to any juice. Broccoli is also a good appetite suppressor.

How many days to detox?
If you have never detoxed before, you may want to start with a three-day plan. If you regularly drink green juices, or have done a plan before, or maybe you eat a lot of raw food, then this detox can be five days.

Preparation
Shop for your ingredients two days before. Stock up on lemons and herbal teas. Make the smoothies and juices a day before to help you keep to the plan.

Schedule
There are six smoothies to consume each day. Start the morning with a nutrient-dense smoothie, break it up with the cleanser, and end with a nut milk to help prevent you from being hungry in the evening. You don't need to drink your smoothie in one go; you can happily sip each one if you prefer. I find a wide straw very helpful.

Daily plan
Repeat this schedule every day.

Smoothie 1: 8 am
Smoothie 2 (the cleanser): 11 am
  (see page 12)
Smoothie 3: 1 pm
Smoothie 4: 3 pm
Smoothie 5: 5 pm
Smoothie 6: 7:30 pm

You don't need to stick to these times, but allow two hours of no consuming before bed. Drink water throughout the day, and if you feel like a tea, try herbal or green tea.

MORNING GRAPEFRUIT: SMOOTHIE 1

Makes about 1¼ cups

YOU NEED

1 grapefruit, peeled • 1 apple, cored and chopped
2 handfuls kale • 5 mint leaves

Add all of the ingredients into the blender with ⅓ to ½ cup of filtered water. Blend until smooth, then pour into a sieve set over a bowl. Help the juice through by pressing gently with a rubber spatula or wooden spoon.

This is bursting with vitamin C, contributing to a healthy immune system.

HS *Hunger Suppressing*   **V** *Vitamin Enhancing*   **D** *Digestion Boosting*

AVOCADO FEAST: SMOOTHIE 3

Makes about 2 cups (drink 1 cup per day)

YOU NEED
1 avocado, peeled and pitted • Juice of ½ lime • 2 sprigs parsley • 1 apple, cored
5 mint leaves • ½ cucumber • A handful of seedless green grapes

---

Add all of the ingredients to the blender with 1¼ cups of filtered water.
Blend until smooth.

This delicious smoothie is rich in vitamins K, C, and E.

BR *Blood Regulating* PE *Protein Enriching* S *Strengthening*

BRAVE BROCCOLI: SMOOTHIE 4

Makes about 1¼ cups

YOU NEED

4 broccoli florets • ¼ baby watermelon, peeled and seeded

3 radishes • ⅓ to ½ cup of coconut water

Add all of the ingredients to the blender. Blend until smooth, then pour into a sieve set over a bowl. Help the juice through by pressing gently with a rubber spatula or wooden spoon.

Bursting with vitamins, this smoothie will help to improve your cardiovascular functioning.

HS *Hunger Suppressing* **BF** *Bacteria Fighting* **BB** *Blood Building*

SPIRULINA SHAKE: SMOOTHIE 5

Makes about 1²/₃ cups

YOU NEED

1 teaspoon spirulina powder • 2 handfuls spinach • 1 apple, cored
½ cucumber • 4 sprigs parsley

Add all of the ingredients to the blender with ⅓ to ½ cup of filtered water. Blend until smooth, then pour into a sieve set over a bowl. Help the juice through by pressing gently with a rubber spatula or wooden spoon.

This is highly nutritious and particularly good for brain function.

BR *Blood Regulating* **PE** *Protein Enriching* **V** *Vitamin Enhancing*

CINNAMON AND CASHEW MILK: SMOOTHIE 6

Makes about 1⅓ cups

YOU NEED

3½ ounces cashew nuts • 1 teaspoon ground cinnamon

2 medjool dates, pitted • 1 teaspoon agave nectar

Add all of the ingredients to a blender with 1¼ cups of filtered water. Blend until smooth, then pour into a sieve set over a bowl. Help the nut milk through by pressing gently with a rubber spatula or wooden spoon.

This helps control blood sugar levels and is a great anti-inflammatory.

BR *Blood Regulating* **C** *Calming* **H** *Healing*

JANUARY DETOX

After burning the candle at both ends and
overindulging on all things delicious, you
might feel that your body is craving some tender
loving care. Often after the festive season we feel
even more tired, our skin is puffy, and our waistline
has decided to expand a little. Well, this plan is
a great way to start the year and to get your body
reignited, feeling full of energy, and raring to go.

Good foods to help with all-around health

Beets
Beets are a great vegetable for a juice, as they are a natural sweetener. Full of folic acid, potassium, magnesium, and iron as well as vitamins A, B-6, and C, beets naturally boost your stamina.

Blueberries
These little fruits pack a powerful nutritional punch. Full of vitamins K and C, blueberries help boost your immune system.

Chia seeds
These black seeds (which you can also buy as an oil) are native to Mexico and Guatemala. They are packed full of nutrients that can have an important effect on the body and brain. Loaded with antioxidants, full of protein, and high in omega-3 fatty acids, these seeds are becoming popular. Chia seed oil can be found online, and is a great way of adding chia seeds to a smoothie.

How many days to detox?
This is a five-day detox plan, but if you haven't detoxed before, I recommend three days for your first time.

Preparation
Shop for your ingredients two days before. Stock up on lemons and herbal teas. Make the smoothies and juices a day before to help you keep to the plan.

Schedule
There are six smoothies to consume each day. Start the morning with a nutrient-dense smoothie, break it up with the cleanser, and end with a nut milk to help prevent you from being hungry in the evening. You don't need to drink your smoothie in one go; you can happily sip each one if you prefer. I find a wide straw very helpful.

Daily plan
Repeat this schedule every day.

Smoothie 1: 8 am
Smoothie 2 (the cleanser): 11 am
  (see page 12)
Smoothie 3: 1 pm
Smoothie 4: 3 pm
Smoothie 5: 5 pm
Smoothie 6: 7:30 pm

You don't need to stick to these times, but allow two hours of no consuming before bed. Drink lots of water; I recommend 6 to 8 cups a day.

CHIA WAKE-UP: SMOOTHIE 1

Makes about 1½ cups

YOU NEED

3 handfuls blueberries • 1 orange, peeled • 2 small carrots
4 broccoli florets • 1 tablespoon chia seed oil

Add all of the ingredients to the blender with ⅔ cup of filtered water. Blend until smooth, then pour into a sieve set over a bowl. Help the juice through by pressing gently with a rubber spatula or wooden spoon.

This is full of omega-3 fatty acids, which help to reduce inflammation.

E *Energizing* **D** *Digestion Boosting* **BS** *Blood Sugar Stabilizing*

SPINACH BOOST: SMOOTHIE 3

Makes about 1 cup

YOU NEED

1 celery stalk • 2 handfuls baby spinach

A small bunch of parsley • ⅓ pineapple, peeled and cut into chunks

Add all of the ingredients to the blender with ⅓ to ½ cup of filtered water. Blend until smooth, then pour into a sieve set over a bowl. Help the juice through by pressing gently with a rubber spatula or wooden spoon.

Full of antioxidants, this will give an overall boost to your health.

V Vitamin Enhancing *RJ* Rejuvenating *A* Anti-inflammatory

ENERGY BEET: SMOOTHIE 4

Makes about 1 cup

YOU NEED

1 apple, cored • 1 carrot • 2 small beets

A sprig of mint • 1 lemon, peeled • A thumb-sized piece of ginger

---

Add all of the ingredients to the blender with ⅔ cup of filtered water. Blend until smooth, then pour into a sieve set over a bowl. Help the juice through by pressing gently with a rubber spatula or wooden spoon.

This is a great liver cleanser to help eliminate toxins from the blood.

ME *Mineral Enhancing* **SB** *Stamina Boosting* **BE** *Blood Enhancing*

BLUE MOON: SMOOTHIE 5

Makes about 1½ cups

YOU NEED

3 handfuls blueberries • 1 orange, peeled

3 handfuls kale • ½ cucumber • 1 teaspoon spirulina powder

Add all of the ingredients to the blender with ⅔ cup of filtered water. Blend until smooth, then pour into a sieve set over a bowl. Help the juice through by pressing gently with a rubber spatula or wooden spoon.

This is full of antioxidants to give a boost to your heart.

I Immune Boosting S Strengthening P Purifying

Copyright © 2016 by Hachette Livre (Marabout)

All rights reserved.
Published in the United States by Ten Speed Press, an imprint of the
Crown Publishing Group, a division of Penguin Random House LLC, New York.
www.crownpublishing.com
www.tenspeed.com

Ten Speed Press and the Ten Speed Press colophon are registered trademarks
of Penguin Random House LLC.

Originally published in French in France as *Super Smoothies: La Bible* by Marabout,
a member of Hachette Livre, Paris, in 2016. Copyright © 2016 by Hachette Livre
(Marabout). This edition was subsequently published in slightly different form
in Australia by Hachette Australia, an imprint of Hachette Australia Pty. Limited,
Sydney, in 2016.

Library of Congress Cataloging-in-Publication Data is on file with the publisher.

Trade Paperback ISBN: 978-0-399-57935-6
eBook ISBN: 978-0-399-57936-3

Printed in China

Design by Alice Chadwick
Photography by Deirdre Rooney

10 9 8 7 6 5 4 3 2 1

First American Edition

ACKNOWLEDGMENTS

I would like to thank everyone who worked on *Super Smoothies* along with
Marabout: Catie Ziller, Kathy Steer, and Alice Chadwick. Also a big thank-you to
Deirdre Rooney for your lovely photos as always. Thanks to Poppy Campbell and
Louisa Chapman-Andrews for whizzing the machine incessantly on the shoot.
And finally, a big thanks to my detox testers; you have been brilliant.